BEYOND TITLES

Unlocking True Leadership from the Inside Out

BY

Nasr Saleh

Table of Contents

INTRODUCTION

Have you ever walked into a room and felt the air crackle with an almost tangible energy? Not because of some high-powered CEO or celebrity, but because someone emanated an aura of genuine presence, a kind of quiet authority that drew you in effortlessly. They listened with their eyes, spoke with conviction, and made you feel like you were the only person in the world. **That, my friend, is a leader.**

And guess what? **You are one too.**

Forget the dusty boardrooms and corner offices. Leadership isn't a title or a position bestowed upon you from above; it's a fire ignited within, a force of nature unleashed from the depths of your being. It's about taking ownership of your journey,igniting your spirit, and guiding others in the same way a lighthouse cuts through the darkest storm. In the world of sales,it's the difference between pushing products and creating lifelong customers, between transactional interactions and transformative relationships. It's about **understanding before selling, connecting before convincing.**

This book isn't about climbing corporate ladders or barking orders. It's about rewiring your mindset, embracing empathy as your superpower, and understanding that true leadership starts with understanding **yourself**. We'll dive deep into the well of your potential, uncovering the courage, resilience, and strategic brilliance that lies hidden beneath the surface.We'll explore the art of emotional intelligence, learning to navigate the intricate dance of human connection with grace and finesse.

Whether you're a seasoned veteran with battle scars etched into your soul or a wide-eyed newbie taking your first tentative steps into the arena, this book is your guide. We'll dispel the myths that leadership is an elite club, reserved for the chosen few. We'll smash the misconception that it's about titles or positions, and instead illuminate the truth: **leadership is about the fire in your heart and the way you light up the world around you.**

So, buckle up and prepare to embark on a journey of self-discovery. We're going to rewrite the rules of sales, redefine leadership in the context of human connection, and unlock the boundless potential that lies dormant within every single one of us. Remember, this isn't just about closing deals; it's about creating a ripple effect of inspiration, leaving a legacy of trust, and building **relationships that last long after the sale is done.**

This is no ordinary sales book. This is your manifesto, your battle cry, your invitation to step into the arena and unleash your inner leader. Are you ready to lead from within and sell from the heart? Let's begin.

CHAPTER 1: SYMPHONY OF SILENCE

The fluorescent lights hum like cicadas in a summer night, a monotonous buzz that permeates the conference room. But beneath the predictable drone, a different energy shimmers – an anticipation that dances on the edges of nervous curiosity. This isn't the tense silence before a high-stakes pitch, nor the forced joviality of a networking breakfast. No, this is the hush of possibility, the expectant silence woven from unspoken trust and genuine human connection.

In the center of this expectant pause stands Sarah. Forget the crisp power suits and practiced pitches of your stereotypical salesperson; Sarah's magnetism radiates from a quieter place. Her voice, warm and unhurried, paints not a canvas of features and statistics, but a dream of hopes, anxieties, and aspirations shared by every face turned towards her. She delves into their hearts, listening not just with ears, but with empathetic eyes that mirror the emotions she evokes. Each shared nod, each knowing smile, speaks volumes without a single word uttered.

This, my friend, is the symphony of silence – the unspoken language of leadership resonating in the space between words. It's a harmony born of genuine connection, not forced persuasion. And guess what? Sarah isn't some elusive sales guru or motivational maestro. She's you. Or the version of you waiting to be unleashed.

For far too long, sales has been relegated to a battlefield, a gladiatorial arena where only the loudest, sharpest, and most aggressive survive. But what if this narrative is a mere shadow play, a distorted picture painted by movies and outdated sales manuals? What if the key to unlocking true sales mastery lies not in brute force, but in a quieter, more potent power – the power of empathy, understanding, and genuine human connection?

This chapter is your invitation to rewrite the script. It's a call to ditch the outdated notions of the "pushy salesman" and step into your role as a leader, not in some distant future, but here and now. We'll embark on a journey together, dismantling the myths that shackle you and uncovering the potent force of inner leadership that resides within.

But first, let's shatter the biggest myth of them all: that leadership is a title or a position.

Leadership isn't some gilded crown bestowed upon you by an unseen hand. It's a fire ignited within, a wellspring of courage and authenticity bubbling to the surface. It's not about barking orders from a corner office or lording over a team from your ivory tower. It's about taking ownership of your journey, setting your own compass, and inspiring others to navigate the vast unknown with you.

Leadership, in its purest form, is about making a difference, leaving a footprint of positive impact on the world around you, and igniting the spark of greatness in those you encounter. And guess what? You have the capacity to do all of that, right now, in the very role you play: sales.

Think about it. Every day, you have the opportunity to connect with people, to delve into their dreams and challenges, and to guide them towards solutions that can truly transform their lives. You have the power to build relationships built on trust and mutual respect, to create value that far surpasses the product or service you're offering.

That's leadership in action.

Now, you might be thinking, "But I'm not a CEO, I'm not a manager, I'm just a salesperson."

And that's precisely where you're wrong. Leadership isn't about titles or positions; it's about mindset, about the way you carry yourself, about the impact you make on those around you.

A true leader isn't defined by their authority, but by their ability to empower others, to ignite their potential, and to create a space where everyone feels valued and heard. So, how do you tap into this well of empathy, understanding, and strategic brilliance that lies hidden beneath the surface? How do you unleash the symphony of silence within yourself?

That's what the rest of this chapter is all about. We'll dive deep into the following areas:

Embracing Empathy as Your Superpower: We'll explore the art of emotional intelligence, learning to navigate the intricate dance of human connection with grace and finesse. This includes understanding basic human emotions, recognizing nonverbal cues, and building rapport through active listening.

Unlocking Your Strategic Brilliance: We'll delve into the world of strategic thinking, helping you craft winning sales strategies that are tailored to the unique needs and motivations of your clients. This involves understanding customer personas, identifying pain points, and presenting solutions that address those needs authentically.

Leading by Example: We'll showcase the real-life stories of everyday heroes who have cultivated their inner leadership and achieved extraordinary results in the sales field. You'll be inspired by examples of

LEADING BY EXAMPLE: EVERYDAY SYMPHONY CONDUCTORS

The Maestro of Micro-transactions: Meet Alex, the barista who transformed the sterile coffee shop into a community hub. He learned his customers' names, remembered their orders, and engaged in genuine conversations about their days. Alex led by example, creating a welcoming atmosphere where regulars felt like family, all while exceeding sales targets through genuine human connection.

The Silent Sales Warrior: Maria, the quiet IT technician, never needed a booming voice to command respect. She led by listening intently, patiently deciphering tech woes, and explaining solutions in simple terms. Her empathy and meticulous attention to detail earned her not just loyal clients, but dedicated advocates who spread the word of her exceptional service.

The Unlikely Influencer: David, the unassuming

accountant, turned budgeting sessions into life-changing conversations. He understood his clients' anxieties and aspirations, guiding them towards financial goals with honesty, humor, and practical advice. David's leadership lay not in spreadsheets, but in empowering his clients to take control of their financial futures, earning their trust and exceeding revenue expectations.

These are just a few whispers in the symphony of silence, testaments to the power of everyday leadership in action. They prove that greatness doesn't require a podium or a corner office; it thrives in the quiet moments of connection, understanding, and genuine human exchange.

Building Your Leadership Chorus:
Now, it's your turn to take the stage. Here are some practical steps you can take to cultivate your inner leader and build your own leadership chorus:

- **Sharpen your listening skills:** Practice active listening, giving your full attention to your clients and colleagues. Pay attention to their words, their body language, and the emotions bubbling beneath the surface.
- **Develop your emotional intelligence:** Learn to recognize and understand your own emotions, as well as the emotions of those around you. This will allow you to respond with empathy and grace, fostering trust and connection.
- **Ask empowering questions:** Go beyond surface-level inquiries. Dig deeper, ask questions that spark insightful conversations and reveal your clients' true needs and motivations.
- **Offer solutions, not sales pitches:** Shift your focus from pushing products to providing

genuine value. Understand your clients' challenges and tailor your solutions to address their specific needs, not just your bottom line.

- **Celebrate small victories:** Recognize and acknowledge every step forward, both yours and your clients'. This builds momentum and reinforces the positive impact you're making.

Remember, the symphony of silence takes practice. There will be stumbles, missed notes, and moments of doubt. But just like any musician, the true leader perseveres, honing their skills, refining their approach, and eventually finding their unique rhythm.

So, step onto the stage, raise your voice, and join the chorus. The world needs your empathy, your understanding, and your spark of inspiration. Start leading by example today and watch as the whispers of your quiet leadership build into a symphony of positive change, one genuine connection at a time.

CHAPTER 2:
UNTAMED GARDEN

Imagine you stumble upon a forgotten plot of land, tucked away on the outskirts of town. No manicured lawns or sculpted hedges here, just a riot of untamed beauty – wildflowers bursting through cracked pavement, rambling ivy scaling a crumbling brick wall, and a gnarled oak casting dappled shadows over the sun-warmed earth. This, my friend, is a metaphor for your inner potential, a fertile landscape teeming with the seeds of leadership waiting to be coaxed into life.

Forget the shiny suits and scripted pitches; true leadership isn't found in external trappings, but in the rich soil of your own being. It's not about a singular, pre-packaged seed you can buy at the store; it's a vibrant quilt woven from threads of courage, resilience, empathy, and strategic thinking, each a unique flower flourishing in your own sunlight and rain.

And guess what? You already have them all nestled within that untamed garden, even if they're currently buried beneath layers of self-doubt and overgrown with the stubborn weeds of limiting beliefs. This chapter is your trusty trowel and watering can, your guide to unearthing that inner garden and helping those leadership seeds blossom into their full potential.

First, we'll embark on a gentle reconnaissance mission. We'll wade through the tangled undergrowth of your self-beliefs, gently pulling out the roots of self-doubt that whisper you're not good enough, not strong enough, not worthy enough. Remember, leadership isn't about some unattainable ideal; it's about embracing your imperfections and using them as steppingstones to growth. Think of those "weeds" as compost, providing rich nutrients for your leadership seeds to thrive.

Next, we'll loosen the soil with self-awareness. Picture yourself digging deep, turning over the earth with curiosity and care. We'll unearth your strengths and weaknesses, your passions and fears. What sets your soul ablaze? What makes your heart sing? Understanding yourself is the foundation upon which you build your unique leadership style, a style that blooms true and authentic to who you are. Think of this self-awareness as tilling the soil, preparing it for the seeds you'll plant.

Now, let's plant the seeds of courage. This isn't about reckless bravado; it's about carefully placing seeds of calculated risk, facing your fears with quiet determination, and learning from the inevitable tumbles and falls. Remember, every fall can be a springboard to soaring higher. Think of planting these seeds as nurturing the tiny shoots of courage that will someday help you stand tall and lead with confidence.

Water them with the life-giving rain of resilience. The

path to leadership is rarely paved with rose petals. There will be setbacks, rejections, and moments when the sky seems to refuse to open up. But just like wildflowers weather storms and bloom again, you too can cultivate the resilience to bounce back stronger and wiser, your roots growing deeper with each challenge overcome. Think of this resilience as the rain that nourishes your courage seeds, enabling them to grow sturdy and strong.

Don't forget to fertilize with the rich compost of empathy. Leadership isn't about barking orders from a distant mountaintop; it's about connecting with your people on a human level, nurturing the fertile ground of shared understanding. Develop your emotional intelligence, learn to listen with your heart, and cultivate the ability to truly see and understand the needs and aspirations of those around you. Think of this empathy as the compost that enriches the soil, nurturing not just your own leadership seeds, but those of everyone you connect with.

Finally, nurture the seedlings with the sunshine of continuous learning. Never stop growing, never stop challenging yourself. Read voraciously, explore uncharted territories, ask uncomfortable questions, and surround yourself with individuals who inspire and motivate you. Every new skill, every piece of knowledge, adds another vibrant flower to your inner garden. Think of this continuous learning as the sunshine that keeps your leadership seeds growing tall and strong, reaching towards the light of fulfillment and potential.

Remember, cultivating your inner leadership garden is a lifelong journey, not a one-time task. There will be days when the sun seems scarce, and the weeds threaten to take over. But don't despair. Stay committed, tend to your garden with care, and trust that over time, you'll witness the most magnificent bloom: the blossoming of your authentic leadership self.

CHAPTER 3: SYMPHONY OF SMILES

The raindrops outside drum a relentless rhythm against the windowpane, blurring the line between the concrete jungle and the weeping sky. Inside the office, a different kind of symphony unfolds – a delicate concerto of unspoken desires and hesitant trust. You sit across from Alex, a potential client whose eyes flicker with hope and hesitation like fireflies caught in a storm. He needs your product, you know, but something unspoken lingers between you, a wall of guardedness waiting to be breached.

This, my friend, is the precipice of the symphony of smiles – a delicate concerto where empathy conducts, and trust becomes the currency. Forget the sterile scripts and polished pitches; here, you're dancing to the music of human connection, a melody woven from unspoken desires and shared anxieties.

Ditch the robotic rigidity of "selling." Instead, step into Alex's shoes, feel the weight of his worries, and resonate with the melody of his unspoken anxieties. Become a detective of the human heart, reading the subtle score played out in body language, the tremolo of uncertainty in his voice, the flickering glint of excitement when you touch upon a specific feature.

Silence hangs heavy in the air, not as an awkward void, but as an invitation to share. Observe first, speak later. Watch the way he fidgets with his pen, the shadows of doubt clouding his eyes. Is it the price that haunts him? Or perhaps the perceived complexity of your offering? Let the silence linger, an echo of your patient understanding.

Then, delve into the deeper waters of "why" and "how." Toss away the shallow yes/no traps and cast open-ended lines: "What keeps you up at night, Alex?" or "What would an ideal solution look like for you?" These questions are your gateway to his world, allowing you to glimpse the hopes and fears that drive him.

Listen not just with your ears, but with your heart. Tune into the emotions simmering beneath the surface. Does his voice tremble with worry? Does a flicker of excitement light up his face when you discuss a specific feature? Be present, engaged, truly hear what he's saying, both verbally and nonverbally.

Mirror his emotions, showing him, you understand by reflecting his feelings. "The uncertainty seems daunting, doesn't it?" or "I hear your frustration, Alex, and I want to assure you..." This validation builds trust, demonstrating that you're not just trying to close a deal, but truly want to partner in his journey.

Speak his language, tailoring your vocabulary and communication style to resonate with his world. Forget the industry jargon and marketing buzzwords. Instead, speak in his terms, using analogies and metaphors that connect with his experience and pain points. Picture yourself painting a vivid picture on his canvas of understanding, using colors he recognizes and shapes that resonate with his needs.

Don't fear the pauses. Silence isn't your enemy; it's a space for reflection and deeper understanding. Let him take his time to process your words, to weigh the options, and to ask clarifying questions. Remember, this isn't a race to the finish line; it's a waltz of mutual discovery.

Now, let's zoom in on the intricate dance unfolding between you and Alex:
He mentions his business, a fledgling coffee shop struggling to stay afloat. You listen intently, noticing the pride in his voice as he talks about his handcrafted latte art. You ask about his biggest challenges, and he confesses his fear of failing, of letting down his loyal customers. You don't launch into a sales pitch; instead, you share your own story – your early struggles as an entrepreneur, the doubts that gnawed at you. You connect with his anxieties, showing him you understand.

As you talk, a subtle shift occurs. The initial guardedness melts away, replaced by a spark of genuine connection. He starts asking questions, leaning in with growing interest. You guide him through the features of your product, showcasing how it can address his specific concerns, not just as a sales pitch, but as a genuine solution to his problems.

When he finally asks about the price, you don't hesitate. You've built trust, understood his needs, and established a relationship. You offer a flexible solution, tailored to his budget and his stage of growth. He pauses, considers, then a hesitant smile creeps across his face. "Let's do it," he says, extending his hand.

The deal is sealed, but the victory lies not in the numbers, but in the symphony of smiles playing out before you. Alex's smile speaks volumes – a smile of relief, of hope renewed, of the shared joy of finding a genuine partner in his journey.

This is the power of emotional salesmanship – the power to transcend transactions and forge connections that leave a lasting impact. It's not about ...It's not about manipulation or trickery, but about authentic empathy, heartfelt understanding, and building trust brick by brick. It's about recognizing that every interaction is a dance, and the music is made not just of words, but of emotions, anxieties, and shared dreams.

This symphony of smiles doesn't play out only in boardrooms and offices. It echoes in classrooms, where passionate teachers ignite sparks of curiosity in their students. It reverberates in hospitals, where compassionate nurses become beacons of hope for ailing patients. It hums in the rhythm of everyday life, in the genuine conversations we share with friends, family, and even strangers.

Remember, the skills you hone in the dance with Alex translate to every arena of your life. The ability to listen actively, to mirror emotions, to tailor your language, and to build trust – these are all universal currencies that can enrich your interactions far beyond the realm of sales.

Here are a few ways to carry the echoes of this symphony into your daily life:

- **Become a student of body language.** Observe the subtle cues that people reveal through their posture, facial expressions, and gestures.
- **Practice active listening.** Give people your full attention, ask clarifying questions, and avoid interrupting.
- **Develop your vocabulary.** Learn to adapt your language to resonate with different audiences and contexts.
- **Offer genuine empathy.** Show people you understand their feelings and share their concerns.
- **Be present in the moment.** Put away your distractions and focus on the person you're interacting with.

By incorporating these elements into your daily life, you can transform even the most mundane interactions into mini symphonies of smiles, leaving a trail of positive connections wherever you go.

Remember, every encounter is an opportunity to connect, to understand, and to build bridges of trust. Step out of your comfort zone, embrace your vulnerability, and let the music of emotional intelligence guide you through the dance of life. The world awaits the rhythm of your compassion, the melody of your understanding, and the symphony of smiles you have the power to create.

CHAPTER 4: DANCING ON HEARTSTRINGS

Close your eyes. Imagine yourself not facing a wall of expectant faces but standing on a stage bathed in the soft glow of shared understanding. Your audience isn't a passive mass to be bombarded with information, but a kaleidoscope of hearts waiting to be stirred, minds yearning to ignite. This, my friend, is the arena of the emotional presentation – a space where vulnerability becomes your strength, and where authentic passion paints a landscape of shared experience.

Forget the bullet points and dry statistics; they belong in sterile spreadsheets, not in this vibrant space where hearts are currency and emotions trump algorithms. Here, you're not just delivering information; you're weaving a world of stories, insights, and experiences that resonate with the deepest threads of your audience's being.

Before you step onto that stage, take a deep breath, shed the armor of formality, and step out of the stiff suit into the skin of your genuine self. Let your personality shine through, your quirks and imperfections adding authenticity to your voice. Remember, people connect not with robots, but with other humans, messy and magnificent in their own right.

Next, ignite the fire within. Find the passion that burns in your core, the purpose that sets your soul ablaze. Let it seep into every word you say, every gesture you make. When you speak with genuine enthusiasm, your audience can't help but catch the sparks. Imagine that passion as a beacon, drawing them closer, inviting them to share in the warmth of your conviction.

Now, pick up your brush – the brush of storytelling. Facts and figures are important, but stories are the paint that brings them to life. Weave anecdotes and personal experiences into your presentation, creating emotional hooks that draw your audience in and make them feel not just informed, but invested. Remember the student who struggled with reading but found joy in your classroom through creative writing projects? Their transformation, recounted with a voice crackling with emotion and eyes glistening with tears of pride, can become a bridge between your experiences and those of the educators in the room, many with similar stories of their own.

Speak the language of the heart, ditching the jargon and technical terms that might alienate your audience. Instead, use metaphors and analogies that connect with their lived experiences, making your message accessible and relatable. Picture yourself explaining a complex scientific principle through the lens of a familiar everyday phenomenon, sparks of understanding flashing in the eyes of your captivated audience.

But remember, true connection is a two-way street. Don't

just speak, listen as deeply as you do. Engage with your audience, respond to their reactions, and use their questions and comments as springboards to delve deeper into your topic. Imagine a lively dialogue unfolding, your words bouncing off the energy of the room, sparking new insights and unexpected connections.

And don't shy away from vulnerability. Share your own struggles, doubts, and triumphs. Your authenticity will disarm your audience, foster trust, and create a space where genuine connection can blossom. Think of that time you faced a seemingly insurmountable challenge in your field, a raw moment of honesty that echoes the anxieties and uncertainties your audience might harbor. Share how you overcame it, not to boast, but to offer them a glimmer of hope, a reminder that even the most inspiring journeys begin with a single step.

Here are some powerful tools to add to your emotional presentation toolbox:

- **Vocal dynamics:** Use variations in pitch, volume, and pace to emphasize key points and evoke emotions. Imagine crafting your voice into an instrument, its notes rising and falling to paint a sonic landscape that mirrors the emotional arc of your presentation.
- **Eye contact:** Connect with individual audience members, making them feel seen and heard. Imagine your gaze as a bridge, reaching out to build a personal connection with each person in the room.
- **Body language:** Use purposeful gestures and facial expressions to reinforce your message and convey authenticity. Imagine your body becoming an extension of your voice, moving in harmony with your words to tell a unified story.

- **Pauses:** Don't be afraid of silence; use it to allow your words to sink in and create anticipation. Imagine these pauses as pregnant moments, pregnant with possibility, where thoughts can linger, and connections can flower.
- **Humor:** A well-placed joke can break the ice, lighten the mood, and endear you to your audience. Imagine yourself using humor as a sprinkle of laughter, adding sweetness and making your message more palatable.

Remember, mastering the art of the emotional presentation isn't about innate talent; it's a skill that blossoms with practice and self-awareness. The more you step outside your comfort zone and embrace vulnerability, the more your presentations will resonate with your audience's hearts.

Now, step onto the stage of your next presentation, not with a script, but with an open heart, a passion to connect, and the courage to and the courage to be your authentic self. You're not just delivering information; you're offering a gift – a gift of vulnerability, of shared wisdom, of a glimpse into the world through your unique lens. And in that offering, you have the power to spark a thousand fires, to ignite a collective desire for change, to move your audience from passive observers to active participants in the symphony of your message.

Remember, every presentation is an opportunity to leave a mark on the world. It's a chance to plant a seed in someone's mind, a seed that might sprout into action, into innovation, into a ripple effect of positive change. So, don't be afraid to bare your soul, to let your passion shine through, to dance on the heartstrings of your audience with every word, every gesture, every beat of your authentic self.

NASR SALEH

!

CHAPTER 5: LEADING THE SALES REBELLION

The sterile air hangs heavy in the conference room, sunlight struggling to pierce through the blinds. Rows of identical chairs offer scant respite from the monotony that permeates the space. Another pitch drone begins, a tired echo of yesterday's tactics, failing to spark even a flicker of interest in the glazed eyes gazing into the middle distance. But in the corner, beneath the hum of fluorescent lights, a seed stirs within you.

This isn't the battlefield of sales you envisioned, the clash of titans wielding sales scripts as bludgeons. No, this suffocating landscape begs for rebellion, a revolution not of volume, but of purpose. You feel it stirring in your gut, a yearning to tear down the sterile walls and cultivate a vibrant sales space, where connection trumps coercion, and empathy fuels success.

This is the call to the Sales Rebellion, not a lone wolf emerging from the shadows, but a symphony of voices rising in unison. It's a movement against the soul-crushing pressure to close deals at any cost, a quiet but resolute stand for client-centricity, understanding, and a shared journey towards growth.

Forget the scripts that choke the life out of genuine conversation. Ditch the robotic patter that leaves a bitter taste of manipulation. Instead, delve into the intricate needs of your client's life. Listen not just with your ears, but with your heart, your eyes seeking the unspoken whispers of need, fear, and aspiration hidden beneath the surface. Understand their "why" before you even dare to hint at your "what."

Challenge the status quo that rewards aggression and exploits vulnerability. Be the thorn in the side of unethical practices, the lone voice questioning tactics that leave scars instead of solutions. Advocate for transparency, for client-centricity, for a dance of negotiation founded on trust and mutual respect.

Arm yourself not with platitudes, but with knowledge gleaned from the trenches of your client's industry. Become a trusted advisor, a navigator in the ever-shifting currents of their market. Don't just know your product; know their story, their challenges, their dreams. Let your expertise be a bridge, not a weapon, guiding them towards informed decisions, not coerced commitments.

Forget the "one size fits all" approach. Ditch the notion of clients as targets and see them as collaborators, fellow travelers on a path to shared success. Identify the goals that bind you, forge genuine partnerships, and turn transactions into transformative journeys. Let your success be not a solitary trophy, but a monument built together, brick by empathetic brick.

This rebellion isn't just about you, the lone wolf howling at the moon. It's about wielding the tools of genuine connection, the weapons of strategic empathy, and the shield of active listening.

Craft stories that captivate, weaving facts and emotions into narratives that resonate with your client's deepest desires. Paint a picture of their transformed future, with your product or service as the brushstroke that illuminates their path.

Become a master of unspoken languages, decoding the subtle cues of body language, the emotional tremors hidden in the pauses between words. Listen not just to what they say, but to the symphony of fears and aspirations that dances just beneath the surface.

Let empathy be your compass, guiding you through the labyrinthine twists and turns of negotiation. Anticipate concerns, address them proactively, and transform the battlefield of pressure into a collaborative dance towards mutually beneficial outcomes.

Lead by example, not with pronouncements, but with actions that echo your values. Let integrity be your compass, transparency your north star, and client-centricity your guiding light. Remember, your actions speak volumes louder than any sales pitch ever could.

Empower your clients to be informed decision-makers, not passive recipients of your expertise. Guide them towards understanding the value you offer, not just the price tag. Let your success be their success, and leave behind a trail of advocates, not disillusioned customers.

Challenge the system from within, even if it means ruffling feathers and facing discomfort. Be the voice of reason against unethical practices, the catalyst for positive change that inspires others to follow suit. Remember, silence fuels injustice; it's your voice that can ignite the rebellion.

Celebrate victories not just as your own, but as

shared triumphs. Acknowledge the contributions of your colleagues, your clients, your ecosystem. Foster a spirit of collaboration, of community, where success is a symphony played by many, not a solo performance.

Remember, the Sales Rebellion isn't a fleeting storm, but a rising tide. It's about transforming the very landscape of sales, brick by empathetic brick. It's about leaving a legacy of trust, of meaningful connections, and of positive change that ripples outwards, one client interaction at a time.

So, step out of the sterile conference room, cast off the shackles of conformity, and join the symphony of the Sales Rebellion. Let your voice rise above the drone, your empathy illuminates the shadows, and your courage pave the way for a future where connection replaces coercion, and collaboration thrives over competition. Imagine a world where clients are not adversaries to be vanquished, but partners in a shared odyssey of growth. Picture conference rooms buzzing with genuine conversations, not the cacophony of closing pitches. Envision sales agreements signed not with trepidation, but with handshakes brimming with mutual respect.

This is the symphony of the Sales Rebellion, a melody composed not of power chords, but of whispers of understanding, strummed on the strings of trust. It's a movement not defined by loud proclamations, but by the quiet acts of everyday heroes – the sales professionals who choose empathy over manipulation, who prioritize value over volume, who see their clients not as targets, but as fellow travelers on the journey towards success.

But this rebellion isn't about overnight revolutions or grand pronouncements. It's a slow burn, a gradual shift in mindset, a daily commitment to the small acts of courage that chip away at the edifice of outdated sales tactics. It's about the barista who remembers your coffee order and asks about your day, building a connection that transcends mere transactions. It's about the financial advisor who patiently walks you through complex financial decisions, empowering you to take control of your future. It's about the tech support specialist who listens to your frustrations without judgment, offering solutions that go beyond the textbook, because they see the human being behind the malfunctioning software.

These are the quiet warriors of the Sales Rebellion, the everyday heroes who are rewriting the narrative one interaction at a time. They are proof that leadership in sales doesn't require a corner office or a booming voice; it thrives in the intimate space of genuine connection, the subtle art of active listening, and the unwavering commitment to understanding the human story behind every sale.

So, join the chorus. Whether you're a seasoned veteran or a wide-eyed rookie, there's a place for you in this symphony. Pick up your instrument, be it the pen that crafts insightful proposals, the phone that fosters understanding over the lines, or simply the open ear that listens without judgment. Let your voice rise above the drone, your empathy illuminate the shadows, and your courage pave the way for a future where sales are not a battlefield, but a bridge, a dance, a shared journey towards mutual enrichment.

Remember, the Sales Rebellion isn't just about individual success; it's about transforming the very landscape of how business is done. It's about building trust, fostering meaningful connections, and leaving a legacy of positive change that ripples outwards, one client interaction, one act of empathy, one note in the symphony of human understanding at a time.

So, what note will you play in this revolution? What chord will you add to the melody of trust and connection? Step into the spotlight, pick up your instrument, and let your voice join the chorus. The Sales Rebellion needs your unique, authentic melody to complete its harmony. Together, we can rewrite the narrative, one sales conversation at a time, and create a symphony of change that echoes through the boardrooms and beyond.

CHAPTER 6:
CLOSING THE DEAL
WITH DISCORD

Forget serene meadows and airy metaphors. The battlefield of sales is paved with cold calls, objection grenades, and the ever-present pressure to close the deal. But fear not, fearless warrior of commerce, for within you lies the potential to be a **conflict ninja**, a master of communication who can disarm even the most skeptical prospect and transform any disagreement into a symphony of collaboration.

Your first weapon? Empathy, the ultimate emotional bazooka disarmer. Forget blasting your features and benefits like a PowerPoint rap gone wrong. Listen, **actually listen**, to your prospect's needs, concerns, and aspirations. Uncover the story behind their objections, the anxieties fueling their resistance. Remember, they're not just another number on your quota list; they're fellow human beings, just trying to navigate their own business jungle.

Next, ditch the barbed wire of arrogance. Sarcasm may feel like a witty way to deflect resistance, but it cuts both ways and leaves everyone bleeding trust points. Opt for honesty delivered with the warmth of a winning smile. Be the sales samurai, not the corporate troll. Think friendly consultant, not pushy pitchman.

Now, because humor is your secret weapon (use it wisely), a well-placed joke can break the ice faster than a free sample at a trade show. Just make sure your aim is true and your target isn't their insecurities. We're aiming for laughter, not pity points. Remember, you're there to build a connection, not roast them like last week's quota miss.

Fourth, acknowledge their objections, even if they sound like nails on a whiteboard. A simple "I understand your concern" or "That's a valid point" can work wonders. It shows you're not just waiting for your turn to unleash your rebuttal like a verbal grenade. You're actually... gasp... trying to **understand them!** Shocking, I know.

And finally, if things get too tense, don't be afraid to hit the pause button. No shame in calling a temporary truce and reconnecting when everyone's calmed down and the air isn't thick enough to slice with a business card. Think of it as a strategic retreat, not a surrender. You live to fight (and close) another day.

Now, onto your arsenal of conflict-diffusing moves:
- **The "Yes, and..." maneuver:** Agree with their objection, then add your solution. Like a culinary fusion artist, create a win-win dish that addresses their concerns and showcases your product's value.
- **The "Can you elaborate?" tactic:** This magic phrase shows you're genuinely interested in their

concerns, not just waiting for your turn to shine. You might even discover new needs you can fulfill! (And bonus points for using it without sounding like a condescending robot.)

- **The "Let's table this for now" break:** Sometimes, stepping away from the battlefield is the smartest move. Take a coffee break, discuss industry trends, or share a funny sales anecdote. Re-engage when the atmosphere is lighter, and trust is rebuilt.
- **The "We both want the same thing" discovery:** Look for shared goals, even if they're hidden. Maybe you both want to save the prospect money, increase efficiency, or achieve a sustainable future. Find that common ground and build your partnership on its foundation.

Remember, navigating tough sales conversations isn't about winning or losing (because let's be honest, you both kind of already lost your dignity in the sales analogy). It's about building trust, finding solutions, and emerging with a new client (and maybe a new friend) intact. So, go forth, conflict ninja, and tango your way through even the most awkward objections. The world needs your communication superpowers, your humor grenades, and your unwavering commitment to not throwing metaphorical punches in the conference room. Just... maybe leave the interpretive dance moves at home. We wouldn't want to cause another office incident, now would we?

Next:
We'll explore specific sales scenarios where you can deploy your conflict-diffusing moves, showcasing different

personalities and approaches to illustrate the principles in action. We'll also delve into diverse situations, such as handling price objections, overcoming competitor arguments, or closing hesitant clients. Get ready to sharpen your sales samurai skills and close more deals, all without breaking a sweat (or resorting to interpretive dance). You've got this!

SCENE 1: THE PRICE-POINT TANGO

Sarah, a bubbly tech salesperson with a knack for understanding customer pains, stands across the polished desk from Mark, a stoic CFO with a budget tighter than a spreadsheet on deadline. Sarah's presenting her revolutionary CRM platform, but the air crackles with the unspoken language of objection: cost.

"The price is... substantial," Mark states, his voice dripping with skepticism. "Can you justify such a high investment compared to competitors?"

Sarah, instead of launching into a defensive spiel, takes a deep breath and channels her inner conflict ninja.

Step 1: Disarm the Sales Bazooka:
"I understand your concern, Mark," she says, her voice calm and confident. "Price is always a factor, and I respect your need to be a good steward of your resources."

Step 2: Ditch the Emotional Barbed Wire:
Mark relaxes slightly, surprised by the lack of sales pressure. "Good," he mutters, leaning back in his chair. "So,

convince me. Why should I choose your platform over the cheaper options?"

Step 3: Collaboration over Competition:
Instead of bad-mouthing the competition, Sarah takes a different approach. She pulls out a chart, not to boast features, but to visualize Mark's specific company needs. "See how your team spends X hours on manual data entry? Our platform automates that, freeing up Y hours for higher-value tasks. That translates to Z dollars in increased productivity each year."

Mark's eyes widen as he follows her calculations. Sarah isn't just selling a product; she's painting a picture of ROI, of solving his pain points in tangible terms.

Step 4: Humor to Seal the Deal:
Sensing the shift in momentum, Sarah adds a touch of humor. "Think of it this way, Mark. Our platform is like a personal trainer for your business. It might cost a bit more than a gym membership, but the results are way more impressive."

A smile cracks Mark's stoic facade. "I like that analogy," he admits. "Alright, Sarah, let's talk details. Can you tailor a package that fits our specific needs and budget?"

And just like that, the potential price clash becomes a collaborative dance. Sarah, by acknowledging Mark's concerns, showcasing value, and adding a dash of humor, transforms a rigid CFO into a willing partner. Soon, they're shaking hands, the deal sealed, not by price alone, but by mutual understanding and the promise of a more efficient, profitable future.

Lesson Learned:

Navigating price objections in sales isn't about brute force or empty promises. It's about demonstrating value, building trust, and finding a win-win solution. Remember, your prospect isn't just a wallet; they're a partner in solving their business challenges. Use empathy, data, and a touch of humor to turn a potential roadblock into a steppingstone towards closing the deal.

SCENE 2: THE FEATURE FEUD

John, a passionate young salesperson with a contagious enthusiasm for innovation, is presenting his company's cutting-edge marketing software to Brenda, a seasoned marketing director known for her meticulous attention to detail. John excitedly showcases the platform's AI-powered analytics, real-time audience insights, and automated campaign customization features.

But Brenda, unimpressed by the bells and whistles, raises a skeptical eyebrow. "These features are interesting, John," she concedes, "but what sets your platform apart from the competition? They offer similar functionalities, often at a lower price point."

John feels the familiar sting of objection but remembers his ninja training. He takes a deep breath and adopts a collaborative stance.

Step 1: Disarm the Sales Bazooka:
"I hear you, Brenda," he says, his voice sincere. "Competition is fierce in this market, and I appreciate your need for clarity."
Step 2: Ditch the Emotional Barbed Wire:
Brenda nods, a hint of curiosity replacing her initial skepticism. "So, tell me, John, how does your platform address pain points that others miss?"

Step 3: Speak Their Language:
John shifts his focus from highlighting features to showcasing specific benefits in Brenda's language. He talks about optimizing campaign ROI, streamlining workflows, and gaining deeper customer understanding – all directly linked to Brenda's key performance indicators.

Step 4: The "Yes, and..." Maneuver:
"And while competitors offer similar functionalities," John adds, "ours are powered by a proprietary AI engine that continuously learns and improves. Imagine your platform getting smarter with every campaign you run, anticipating your needs and suggesting even more effective strategies."

Brenda's eyes gleam with interest. The focus has shifted from a feature war to a discussion of strategic advantage.

Step 5: Offer a Demonstration:
"Want to see it in action, Brenda?" John asks, seizing the momentum. "I can tailor a demo based on your current campaign challenges and show you how our AI can significantly increase your conversion rates."
Brenda nods eagerly. They spend the next hour exploring

the platform together, Brenda's initial resistance melting away as John demonstrates the tangible value proposition beyond the mere features. By the end, she's not just convinced; she's excited to be an early adopter, eager to leverage the platform's unique capabilities to outshine her competitors.

Lesson Learned:
Don't get lost in the feature jungle when facing objections in sales. Speak your prospect's language, connect your features to their specific needs, and showcase the unique value that sets you apart. Remember, it's not about boasting flashy features; it's about solving their problems and helping them achieve their goals in a better way. By employing empathy, strategic communication, and a willingness to tailor your approach, you can transform even the most feature-focused feud into a fruitful partnership.

Why mastering difficult conversations makes you a sales leader:
The ability to navigate tough sales conversations like the ones you witnessed with Sarah and John isn't just a valuable skill; it's a defining trait of true sales leadership.

Here's why:
1. **Builds Trust and Credibility:** When you approach objections with empathy, humor, and genuine collaboration, you build trust with your prospects. They see you not as a pushy salesperson, but as a trusted advisor, someone who understands their needs and is genuinely invested in their success. This trust is the foundation of long-term partnerships and repeat business.

2. Uncovers Hidden Opportunities: By actively listening to concerns and objections, you unearth valuable insights into your prospect's challenges and priorities. This allows you to tailor your offering and present solutions that address their specific needs, uncovering opportunities you might have otherwise missed.

3. Elevates Negotiation Skills: Difficult conversations are, in essence, mini negotiations. Mastering the art of disarming resistance, finding common ground, and reaching mutually beneficial agreements equips you to handle high-stakes negotiations with clients, partners, and even within your own organization.

4. Empowers and Inspires Your Team: As a leader, your approach to conflict sets the tone for your team. By demonstrating how to handle objections with calm, professional resilience, you inspire your team members to follow suit. This creates a culture of open communication, constructive collaboration, and ultimately, higher sales performance.

5. Positions You as a Strategic Partner: Forget closing deals through sheer persistence. Today's buyers want partners who understand their business, anticipate their needs, and can navigate challenges collaboratively. By mastering difficult conversations, you position yourself as a strategic partner, not just a product peddler. This enhances your value proposition and opens doors to long-term, mutually beneficial business relationships.

Remember, leadership isn't about avoiding conflict; it's about navigating it with skill and grace. By embracing difficult sales conversations as opportunities for growth, collaboration, and trust-building, you not only close deals, but also solidify your position as a true leader in the ever-evolving landscape of sales.

So, transform those sales objections into steppingstones on your path to sales leadership! The world needs your communication superpowers, your humor grenades, and your unwavering commitment to finding win-win solutions, even in the heat of the sales battlefield. Just remember, leave the interpretive dance moves at home (unless you're closing a deal with a mime convention, of course).

CHAPTER 7: THE RIGHT WAY, THE FAST WAY

Forget sprinting through your to-do list in a blur of caffeine and stress. Forget the endless cycle of crossed-off tasks and lingering guilt. True productivity isn't just about getting things done; it's about getting the right things done, the right way, and feeling fulfilled in the process. So, grab your metaphorical yoga mat and ditch the hamster wheel. We're embarking on a journey towards mindful efficiency, where purpose meets passion, and results speak volumes without sacrificing your sanity.

The Importance of Doing Things the Right Way:
In today's hustle culture, "doing things the right way" often gets swept aside in the relentless pursuit of "just getting it done." But here's the secret: taking shortcuts and sacrificing quality only creates bigger problems down the line. Sloppy work leads to rework, missed deadlines, and frustrated clients. Rushed decisions breed costly mistakes and missed opportunities.

Instead, consider the long-term impact of your actions. Ask yourself:

- Is this the best use of my time and energy?
- Am I sacrificing quality for speed, and will it come back to bite me later?
- Are my actions aligned with my personal values and bigger goals?

Remember, true achievement lies not just in crossing things off a list, but in building a meaningful career and a life that aligns with your values.

Mastering Productivity with Purpose:
Now, onto the magic formula:

1. Know Your "Why": Before you dive into tactics, connect with your internal compass. What are your aspirations? What motivates you? Aligning your actions with your deeper purpose fuels intrinsic motivation and makes the daily grind feel less like drudgery and more like a meaningful journey. I credit Simon Sinek for coining "The Know Your Why" Philosophy, it is truly great.

2. Prioritize Ruthlessly: Not all tasks are created equal. Learn to differentiate between urgent and important, between busywork and game-changers. Invest your time and energy in activities that have the most significant impact on your goals. ruthlessly eliminate timewasters and distractions.

3. Embrace Focus: Multitasking is a myth. Your brain can only truly focus on one thing at a time. Embrace single tasking, eliminate distractions, and create a space conducive to deep work. You'll be amazed at how much more you can accomplish in less time.

4. Power Up Your Habits: Small, daily habits have a cumulative effect on your productivity. Build routines that support your focus, well-being, and energy levels. Exercise, healthy eating, and mindful practices can be your secret weapons in the battle against burnout.

5. Celebrate the Process: Productivity isn't just about the destination; it's about the journey. Celebrate the small wins, acknowledge your progress, and recognize the effort you put in. This positive reinforcement helps you stay motivated and engaged in the long run.

Remember:

- Perfectionism is the enemy of progress. Aim for "good enough" instead of "perfect" and move on with confidence.
- Delegate and collaborate. You don't have to do everything yourself. Leverage the strengths of others and free up your time for higher-value tasks.
- Learn to say no. Don't overload yourself with commitments that drain your energy and distract you from your goals.
- Take breaks and recharge. Schedule downtime for rest, recreation, and creative rejuvenation. A well-rested mind is a productive mind.

By embracing the principles of doing things the right way and mastering productivity with purpose, you can ditch the hamster wheel and step onto a path of meaningful accomplishment, lasting fulfillment, and a life that truly reflects your values. So, go forth, mindful achievers, and claim your power to be productive, purposeful, and stress-free in the best way possible!

Next:

The Cracked Code of Creativity (Enhanced):

- **Forest:** This app gamifies focus by virtually planting a tree that grows as you remain productive. Seeing your digital forest flourish can be a powerful motivator to stay in the zone.
- **Headspace:** Short mindfulness exercises within the app can help you clear your mind and access deeper creative wells.
- **Miro:** A collaborative brainstorming tool perfect for capturing and building upon fleeting ideas with your team.

The Tamed Inbox Tango (Enhanced):

- **Todoist:** A robust to-do list app allows you to organize tasks by project, priority, and due date, ensuring nothing falls through the cracks.
- **Freedom:** This app temporarily blocks distracting websites and apps, enabling you to focus on deep work without digital temptations.
- **Unroll.me:** Aggregates daily emails from specific senders into concise digests, reducing your inbox clutter and making email more manageable.

Beyond the Scenes:

- **RescueTime:** Tracks time spent on different websites and apps, helping you identify and address hidden productivity drains.
- **Evernote:** A digital notebook to capture fleeting ideas, project notes, and research materials, keeping everything organized and

easily accessible.

- **Google Calendar:** An essential tool for scheduling tasks, meetings, and breaks, ensuring your day is structured and predictable.

Remember, these are just a few suggestions. Explore different apps and tools to find what resonates with your unique style and needs.

Bonus Tip: Regularly declutter your digital workspace. Delete unused apps, unsubscribe from unnecessary emails, and organize your files for improved clarity and focus.

With the right blend of mindful practices, helpful apps, and tailored strategies, you can transform your workday into a symphony of efficiency and fulfillment. Remember, the key is to embrace conscious action, prioritize well-being, and make technology work for you, not the other way around. Now go forth, mindful achievers, and conquer your productivity goals!

CHAPTER 8:
CULTIVATING CALM

The modern workplace can be a pressure cooker. Tight deadlines, demanding expectations, and the constant hum of technology can take a toll on even the most resilient individuals. In this chapter, we'll explore how mindfulness and mental health practices can transform your work environment, fostering greater well-being, collaboration, and even productivity.

Mindfulness: More Than Just a Buzzword

Mindfulness isn't simply about sitting cross-legged chanting "om." It's about cultivating present-moment awareness, non-judgmental observation of your thoughts and emotions, and an acceptance of what is. In the workplace, this translates to:

- **Reduced stress and anxiety:** By noticing and regulating your emotional responses, you can defuse stressful situations and remain calm under pressure.
- **Improved focus and concentration:** A mindful mind is a focused mind, allowing you to tackle tasks with greater clarity and efficiency.
- **Enhanced communication and**

collaboration: Mindful listening and communication foster deeper understanding and empathy, leading to more productive and harmonious interactions with colleagues.

- **Greater self-awareness:** By tuning into your internal landscape, you can identify your strengths and weaknesses, leading to greater personal and professional growth.

Bringing Mindfulness to Your Day:

No need for meditation retreats or incense burners. Simple practices can integrate mindfulness into your workday:

- **Start with your breath:** Take a few minutes each day to focus on your breath, allowing your mind to come to rest in the present moment.
- **Mindful commute:** Instead of checking your phone, observe the sights and sounds around you, cultivating awareness of your surroundings.
- **Mindful eating:** Focus on the taste, texture, and smell of your food, savoring each bite without distractions.
- **Tech breaks:** Schedule regular breaks away from screens to allow your mind to refresh and reset.
- **Body awareness:** Take micro-moments throughout the day to check in with your posture, tension levels, and breath.

Mental Health: A Shared Responsibility

Beyond individual practices, creating a supportive workplace culture is crucial for promoting mental health:

- **Encourage open communication:** Normalize conversations about mental health and provide resources for employees seeking support.
- **Promote flexible work arrangements:** Offer

options for remote work, flexible hours, and breaks to reduce stress and accommodate individual needs.

- **Lead by example:** Demonstrate genuine care for employee well-being and model healthy work habits yourself.
- **Celebrate personal development:** Encourage employees to pursue mindfulness and mental health initiatives related to their personal growth.

Remember:

- Mental health is just as important as physical health.
- Taking care of yourself makes you a better colleague, leader, and overall human being.
- Implementing mindfulness and mental health practices can lead to a more positive, productive, and fulfilling work environment for everyone.

Next:

We'll explore specific mindfulness exercises and resources you can implement in your workplace, dive into the role of leadership in promoting mental health and address common challenges in creating a culture of well-being. Stay tuned for continued guidance on making your workplace a haven for both productivity and inner peace!

Imagine stepping into a workplace where the air crackles not with tension, but with a quiet focus. Where colleagues collaborate with genuine empathy, and deadlines are met not with panic, but with calm efficiency. This isn't some utopian dream; it's the reality achievable through mindfulness and mental health practices seamlessly woven into the fabric of your work environment.

Forget the tired notion of mindfulness as a fluffy buzzword reserved for yoga studios. In the workplace, it's a potent tool for:

- **Taming the Stress Kraken:** By simply observing your thoughts and emotions without judgment, you can defuse stressful situations before they boil over. Deep breaths become your superpower, enabling you to respond thoughtfully rather than react impulsively.
- **Sharpening Your Mental Samurai Sword:** A mindful mind is a focused mind. By quieting the internal chatter, you can concentrate on tasks with laser-like precision, boosting your productivity and reducing the dreaded error rate.
- **Building Collaboration Bridges:** Mindful listening and communication foster deeper understanding and empathy, allowing you to connect with colleagues on a human level. Suddenly, brainstorming sessions become symphonies of shared ideas, and conflicts get resolved through open dialogue, not power struggles.
- **Unveiling Your Hidden Treasures:** By tuning into your internal landscape, you discover your strengths and weaknesses with newfound clarity. This self-awareness becomes the compass guiding your personal and professional growth, paving the way for fulfillment and mastery.

Integrating mindfulness into your workday doesn't require drastic changes. Simple practices like mindful commutes, focused lunch breaks, and even a few minutes of deep breathing can work wonders. Encourage colleagues to experiment with walking meetings, silent reflection spaces, or even company-wide meditation sessions.

Remember, small ripples of mindfulness can create a tidal wave of calm in your work environment.

But true transformation goes beyond individual practices. Building a culture of mental health is a shared responsibility, requiring commitment from both leadership and team members. Normalize conversations about mental health, offering resources and support without judgment. Promote flexible work arrangements to reduce stress and accommodate individual needs. Lead by example, demonstrating genuine care for employee well-being and modeling healthy work habits yourself. Celebrate personal development, encouraging employees to explore mindfulness and mental health initiatives that resonate with them.

Remember, a healthy mind isn't a luxury; it's a necessity for a thriving workplace. By prioritizing mental well-being and embracing mindfulness, you create a space where productivity thrives alongside purpose, and success is measured not just by profits, but by the collective happiness and well-being of your team. Go forth, mindfulness warriors, and spread the calm!

The journey towards a calm and productive workplace continues. Now, let's dive into specifics, equipping you with tools and strategies to transform your work environment:

Mindfulness Exercises for Busy Bees:
- **The 5-minute Gratitude Boost:** Before diving into your to-do list, take a moment to list five things

you're grateful for, shifting your mindset to positivity.

- **Mini-Meditations on the Go:** Close your eyes, focus on your breath, and count 10 inhales and exhales during elevator rides or bathroom breaks.
- **The Mindful Meeting Makeover:** Start meetings with a brief silence for everyone to center themselves and encourage active listening by avoiding multitasking.
- **Walking Work Wonders:** Schedule walking meetings or take walking breaks to clear your head, stimulate creativity, and boost energy.
- **Body Scans at your Desk:** Take a few minutes to scan your body, noticing any areas of tension and gently releasing them.

Resources for Your Mindfulness Toolkit:

- **Headspace:** Guided meditations for beginners and advanced practitioners alike.
- **Calm:** A comprehensive app offering meditations, sleep stories, and breathing exercises.
- **Insight Timer:** A free platform with thousands of meditations on various topics and lengths.
- **Mindful Magazine:** Articles, podcasts, and resources to deepen your understanding of mindfulness.
- **Books like "Wherever You Go, There You Are" by Jon Kabat-Zinn and "Mindfulness at Work" by David Dewulf:** Dive deeper into the theory and practice of mindfulness in the workplace.

Leadership: Setting the Tone for Mental Well-being:

- **Open Communication:** Create a safe space for employees to discuss mental health concerns without fear of judgment.
- **Destigmatize Mental Health Days:** Offer paid time off specifically for mental health and encourage its use without guilt.
- **Lead by Example:** Take breaks, practice mindfulness, and prioritize your own well-being to model healthy habits for your team.
- **Promote Work-Life Balance:** Discourage presenteeism and encourage employees to disconnect after work to recharge.
- **Invest in Mental Health Resources:** Offer employee assistance programs, mindfulness training, and access to mental health professionals.

Addressing Common Challenges:

- **Skepticism:** Combat resistance by emphasizing the benefits of mindfulness for both individual and team well-being.
- **Time Constraints:** Offer short, practical exercises that can be easily integrated into busy schedules.
- **Distractions:** Create dedicated spaces for mindful practice and encourage colleagues to respect quiet zones.
- **Budgetary Limits:** Explore free resources and low-cost options for mindfulness training and mental health initiatives.
- **Reluctant Teams:** Start with small, voluntary initiatives and gradually build acceptance and enthusiasm.

Remember, fostering a culture of mindfulness and

mental health is a journey, not a destination. Be patient, persistent, and celebrate every step towards a calmer, more productive, and happier workplace. Together, we can create a new paradigm where success and well-being are not contradictory, but complementary forces shaping a world of work that benefits everyone.

CHAPTER 9: UNMASKING THE LEADER WITHIN

I used to be a champion of the two-act play. Every morning, I'd pull on my "work mask," transforming into the image of unflappable competence. Behind it, the "real me" - the one juggling a toddler meltdown, worrying about my aging parents, and harboring dreams of writing a novel - remained hidden. But this compartmentalization, this illusion of separation, was my downfall. It held me back from becoming the leader I truly desired to be.

Here's why:

Empathy was an act, not an instinct. I could say the right words, offer polite condolences, but I couldn't truly tap into the well of understanding needed to support my team through their personal struggles. Their anxieties felt abstract, distant, because I kept my own tucked away under lock and key. How could I expect them to feel safe confiding in me when I wasn't willing to be vulnerable myself?

Engagement was a mirage. My team saw me as an efficient machine, not a human being. They admired my results, but didn't truly connect with me. This surface-level interaction created a distance that stifled creativity, collaboration, and ultimately, their full potential. How could I inspire them to excel when they only knew a fragment of who I was, a curated persona instead of the whole story?

Success was hollow. Achievements felt fleeting, victories tinged with a sense of emptiness. My "work self" couldn't fully celebrate because it wasn't integrated with the "me" outside the office, the me who longed for more than just numbers on a spreadsheet. How could I lead others towards genuine fulfillment when I myself was chasing an illusion?

The turning point came when I realized the futility of this act. I was exhausting myself playing two roles, and my team was missing out on the best version of me, the leader who could guide them not just with strategy, but with empathy, authenticity, and a shared understanding of the human experience.

So, I took a leap of faith. I started sharing bits of my "real life" - the joys and struggles, the fears and aspirations. I listened more intently to my team's stories, recognizing the reflections of my own vulnerabilities in theirs. I allowed myself to be human, imperfect, and relatable.

The transformation was remarkable. Empathy became genuine, flowing effortlessly from a place of shared understanding. Engagement deepened, with team members stepping out of their comfort zones, bringing their whole selves to the table. Success tasted sweeter, celebrated not just with colleagues, but with the integrated me, the leader and the human, finally united.

Here's what I learned:

- **Leading with vulnerability isn't a weakness, it's a strength.** It creates trust, fosters connection, and empowers others to do the same.
- **Bringing your whole self to work doesn't diminish your professionalism; it expands it.** It allows you to lead with authenticity, inspiring others to be their best selves too.
- **Your personal struggles aren't distractions; they're lessons.** They equip you with empathy, resilience, and a deeper understanding of the human condition, all essential qualities for any leader.

This journey isn't always easy. There will be moments of doubt, whispers of insecurity urging you to retreat behind the mask. But remember, unmasking the leader within is not just about you; it's about creating a work environment where everyone feels seen, valued, and empowered to thrive. It's about fostering a culture of authenticity and empathy, where success is measured not just by profit, but by the collective well-being and growth of its members.

Embrace the full spectrum of your humanity. Share your stories, listen deeply to others, and allow the strings of your life to enrich your leadership. For in embracing your own vulnerability, you unlock the key to unlocking the potential of those around you, and together, pave the way for a future where work isn't just a place to go, but a space to connect, grow, and become the best versions of ourselves, both within and beyond the walls of the office.

Remember, the leader you truly want to be doesn't reside in some distant future, waiting to be revealed. She's already there, hidden within the layers of your "real life." Unmask her and watch her shine.

The journey of embracing your whole self as a leader doesn't stop with introspection and vulnerability. It extends outwards, demanding action and intentionality to create a workplace that reflects this new paradigm. Here's how to move beyond personal revelation and translate it into tangible change:

Building Bridges of Empathy:

- **Normalize open communication:** Encourage team members to share their personal challenges, creating a safe space for honest conversations without judgment.
- **Offer practical support:** Implement flexible work arrangements, childcare resources, or wellness programs that acknowledge the diverse needs of your team.
- **Lead by example:** Model healthy work-life boundaries, take regular breaks, and openly advocate for well-being, demonstrating that prioritizing personal balance doesn't equate to diminished commitment.
- **Celebrate individuality:** Recognize and appreciate the unique experiences, talents, and perspectives that team members bring from their outside lives, appreciating them as integral parts of their professional contributions.

Empowering Through Authenticity:

- **Share your own struggles:** Be transparent about your personal challenges and victories, fostering a sense of shared humanity and inspiring others to be vulnerable themselves.
- **Give meaningful feedback:** Shift from impersonal

critiques to honest, constructive conversations that acknowledge both strengths and areas for growth, focusing on individual development not just performance metrics.

- **Delegate with trust:** Empower team members by delegating meaningful tasks, encouraging ownership, and providing opportunities for them to showcase their unique talents.
- **Focus on purpose beyond profit:** Connect your work to a larger social mission, creating a sense of shared meaning and purpose that motivates and inspires your team beyond mere financial incentives.

Transforming the Workplace Culture:

- **Organize meaningful team-building activities:** Move beyond generic icebreakers and delve into activities that foster deeper connections and understanding of each other's lives and passions.
- **Prioritize mental health initiatives:** Offer mindfulness workshops, stress management resources, and access to mental health professionals, recognizing the interconnectedness of personal well-being and professional performance.
- **Create a space for reflection and growth:** Encourage continuous learning and personal development, not just in technical skills, but also in areas like emotional intelligence, leadership, and self-awareness.
- **Champion work-life balance:** Discourage presenteeism and celebrate successes outside of work, emphasizing the importance of rest, recharging, and pursuing personal fulfillment.

Remember, this journey is a marathon, not a sprint. Building a culture of empathy, authenticity, and well-being takes time and commitment. But every step you take, every vulnerable conversation you initiate, every action you implement to support your team's human needs, is a step towards a brighter future. A future where leadership transcends power dynamics and becomes a collaborative dance of shared humanity, enabling everyone to thrive, both at work and beyond.

Continue moving forward and become the architect of a workplace that nurtures not just productivity, but the full spectrum of human potential. Remember, you are not just transforming your environment; you are transforming yourself, shedding the layers of compartmentalization to emerge as the leader you were always meant to be – whole, authentic, and empowered to guide others towards a more fulfilling future for all.

NASR SALEH: SHINING BRIGHTER, TOGETHER

Forget the fancy titles and lofty expectations. I'm just Nasr, a husband, father of two, and yes, a guy who spends a bit too much time in sales meetings (15 years' worth, to be precise!). But underneath the spreadsheets and product demos, there's a spark, a flicker of hope I desperately want to share.

See, I stumble just like you. My mornings often resemble a controlled chaos symphony, and finding "me time" feels like searching for a unicorn in my laundry basket. But amidst the mess, I discovered a truth: **leadership isn't about having it all figured out; it's about helping others see the light even when it feels dim.**

Maybe it's the faith I hold close, or the infectious laughter of my boys, or the unwavering support of my wife, but something ignites a fire within me. A fire that whispers, "Hey Nasr, there's more to you than this cubicle. Shine a light on someone else's path, even if it's just with a flickering candle."

And that's how I stumbled into writing. Not as some literary genius, mind you, but as a guy with a message: **true leadership isn't a position; it's a way of being.** It's about empathy, seeing the good in someone even when they're covered in metaphorical coffee stains. It's about collaboration, understanding that greatness blooms when we lift each other up. It's about **human connection, realizing that shared stories and genuine laughter are the stuff of real magic.**

I pour this message into my books, like "How to Shine" and this very one, hoping to spark a tiny ember in someone's heart. And let me tell you, the stories I get back? Those are the real magic. People reaching out, sharing how those flickers turned into bonfires, illuminating their own paths and the lives around them. That's what keeps me going, even when the words feel stuck and the self-doubt whispers too loud.

I'm not here to preach or claim some grand expertise. I'm just a man on a journey, inviting you to join me. Let's shed the pretense, share our stumbles and triumphs, and discover the leader within each of us. Let's shine brighter, together.

Want to connect?
Email: nasrsalehstories@gmail.com
LinkedIn: www.linkedin.com/nasrsaleh

Remember, even the smallest light can cast a giant shadow. Let's start casting some beautiful ones, shall we?

Shine on, friends.